SHAME

Understanding and Coping

Portions of the Twelve Steps reprinted with permission of
A.A. World Services, Inc.
A list of works referred to or consulted by the author
appears at the back of the text. Hazelden expresses its
appreciation to those authors and publishers whose materials
have been quoted.
Printed in the United States of America.

Part I: Understanding Shame

Part II: Coping with Shame

Introduction

Recovery from active alcoholism is simple. You just don't drink — that is, you stay away from the first drink, one day at a time. Living as a sober alcoholic, not only maintaining sobriety but progressing in recovery, can prove a bit more complex.

As usual, among those who try to live the program of Alcoholics Anonymous, let me start off by saying sincerely that I write these pages for my sake — to help me stay sober. I hope what you read will help you in your sobriety.

My real name is irrelevant, but I am an alcoholic. Also, toward the end of my drinking, I popped quite a few pills — all legally prescribed, although not all honestly obtained from the trusting doctors I made a hobby of conning.

It wasn't a difficult hobby. We alcoholics develop considerable skill at conning, what with all the practice we get conning ourselves. Besides that, I am one of those over-educated, professionally trained alcoholics who can talk in psychology. Doctors have a hard time labeling us "alcoholic" — about as hard a time as we have ourselves. "Denial" is no respecter of degrees.

Over time, the mounting dishonesties in my life caused it to fall apart. Alcohol and other chemicals no longer killed the pain. In fact, I dimly came to realize that they were adding to it. During my fourth admission for detoxification, a caring physician, a street-tough cop, and a respected clergyman friend all "suggested" treatment for chemical dependency. Having nowhere else to go — my employers and my living companions had both strongly indicated that they would just as soon never see me again — I graciously consented to use the airplane ticket to Minnesota that a former employer generously provided in lieu of severance pay.

For someone so smart, I learned a lot in treatment: complicated concepts like "Easy Does It" and "First Things First." I also absorbed a few things that didn't come packaged in such neat maxims, and it is one of these that I hope to share with you in this booklet. My story reveals that the pain of dishonesty, the trauma of knowing I was not the person I pretended to be and was *supposed to be*, lay at the core of my alcoholism and addiction. After all, who ever heard of a professional person, with degrees and even titles, *needing* a drink?

Fortunately, I met others like me in treatment. And even more fortunately, the first important thing I discovered was that they were "like me" not because of the degrees and titles — some didn't have them — but because they *hurt as humans.* An alcoholic mother or a pill-popping wife or any of a hundred other kinds of people in a thousand different situations can hurt and ache and wrench and clutch inside just as I did — and then can get caught in the trap of trying to soothe that pain with chemicals such as alcohol.

Some people, I learned, can do that — soothe the pain — and get away with it. They seem not to have the physical metabolism or the "physiological x" or the *whatever* that is somehow a part of those of us who become alcoholics. For a brief time, I envied such people. My "Why me's?" oozed self-pity until one crisp fall day as I walked privately, sensuously absorbing the beauties around me, a new — truly sober — way of thinking gently insinuated itself into my mind and feelings.

"Why me?" indeed! Why should I be one of the lucky ones to see the vibrant colors of autumn leaves through unhazed eyes? To hear the breezy rustle of those leaves punctuated by chipmunk chirps and the lap of the waves on the lakeshore and the resounding calls of migrating waterfowl? To smell the clean fall air with its scents of apples and wood-smoke and of the furrowed and harvested good earth preparing for its winter sleep? To feel on my face the occasional sting of a gust of wind

— was that an early snowflake that just pinched my cheek? — and the resilient, grassed path under my feet and the gnarled bark of the wise, aged trees that I rub against in passing. Why should I be one of the lucky ones able to stand before and within all this beauty, to drink it in with *clear* senses, able to confront and to appreciate reality as it is without a curtain of chemicals? Indeed, "Why me?"!

They told me something interesting in treatment: there is a difference between getting sober and staying sober. I pegged my memory of that warning — of that *promise* — on some words of Bill Wilson, co-founder of Alcoholics Anonymous. "Honesty gets us sober but tolerance keeps us sober," Bill once said. Over the years, I have hung a lot on that phrase. But especially, I hang on it whenever I catch myself feeling bad.

In treatment and in early sobriety I began to learn quite a few things about feeling bad. I learned that there were some kinds of feeling bad that I never had to go through again. The physical side, the terrors of withdrawal, headed that list; but it included the worries about behavior during blackouts and other misbehaviors fueled by alcohol. What a simple, liberating truth it was to know that if I didn't drink, I wouldn't get drunk!

Yet there was more to learn about feeling bad. Growing sobriety taught, for example, that there is a vast difference between *feeling* bad and feeling *bad*. That is not, believe me, just a play on words. *Feeling* bad means hurting. The active alcoholic experiences myriad ways of *feeling* bad.

Feeling *bad* is something else. In fact, as we shall see, it is two things else. Feeling *bad* means feeling that there is something wrong with me, about me. One thing I had to learn was that feeling *bad* is different from *feeling* bad, and there are two different kinds of feeling *bad*. Until I learned to tell them apart, getting and staying truly sober was a lot harder. In fact, for me, staying sober at all seemed nearly impossible.

There were two ways, I learned not so quickly, in which even the non-drinking alcoholic could feel *bad*. And until I learned to sort them out, learned to handle each one differently, this non-drinking alcoholic was never able to find even the semblance of true sobriety. There was, I discovered, a real and significant difference between the feeling *bad* of *guilt*, and the feeling *bad* of *shame*. "Guilt" concerned what I *did*. "Shame" was about what I *was*. And there's more: let me try to tell you about it.

Part I:

Understanding Shame

Shame, Guilt or Embarrassment

Shame differs from guilt. For one thing, it is a more troublesome feeling to confront and relieve. Facing up to guilt — the things that we *do* — although it can be painful, is not really difficult. The beginner in Alcoholics Anonymous, for example, finds guilt eased by A.A.'s very First Step, in the admission of powerlessness and unmanageability. As recovery progresses, the alcoholic finds further help in dealing with guilt in the inventory and amendment Steps of the A.A. program. Especially A.A.'s Fourth, Eighth, and Ninth Steps guide us directly to the resolution of guilt.[1]

Facing up to shame — to what we *are* — proves more tricky and, for most of us, more difficult. As with guilt, Alcoholics

Anonymous suggests a solution for shame.* That solution is anticipated in the admission of powerlessness and unmanageability. Steps Five, Six and Seven start the process of resolving shame.[2] But it is Alcoholics Anonymous as a *fellowship* that makes the solution real. I hope, in what follows, to show how; but, first, it is necessary to spend a few moments thinking and talking about those words, "guilt" and "shame."

Neither word is used much nowadays. "Guilt" seems mainly a technical term, used appropriately only by psychiatrists and lawyers. Our modern age so mistrusts any whiff of moralism that most people have become uncomfortable with the term "guilt." "Shame" labors under a different disability. Generally reserved for training children and animals, it suffers mightily from this association with helpless dependency. "Shame" carries echoes of being caught; and, of course, no truly mature person is ever naughty.

Such an understanding of shame contains a trap. I used to think that shame was the same as embarrassment, that it resulted from being seen or caught by someone. As children, we are told to be ashamed of ourselves when we are caught publicly. But even as children, shame results not from being *seen* doing something, but from *what* we are caught doing! Embarrassment, therefore, is not the same as shame, but is the result of one's *shame* being seen.

In my home A.A. group, one oldtimer — a seasoned alcoholic literally grizzled and occasionally crass, but filled with the deep and loving wisdom that comes from long and joyous sobriety — once suggested a thought that, although it offended me at first, made a point that for the sake of my sobriety it seems I had to hear. According to Ben, the words themselves help you

*The opinions expressed are solely those of the author and do not represent A.A. as a whole.

4

to tell embarrassment from shame. "Embarrassed" means being caught "bare-assed." "Bare" means uncovered, and therefore *seen,* but it is *what* is seen, one's *derriere* — the testimony to one's *shame* — that causes embarrassment. "Bare-faced," Ben liked to point out, means the exact opposite of "embarrassed."

As I said, I didn't like Ben's image when I first heard it, but over time I discovered in it a deep wisdom that I now find helpful in handling my shame. For now, let's nail down this important distinction between shame and embarrassment by noting that the sense of shame comes before any sense of being seen by another. Our shame exists in us, in ourselves — indeed, in our very *self,* which is why shame is so important to the discovery of who we *really* are. Other people do not cause our feelings of shame. Rather, as we shall examine in later chapters, in a strange quirk that reveals the treachery of confusing embarrassment and shame, we learn in A.A. that others provide the only true therapy for the discomforts and agonies of shame.

So much for the distinction between shame and embarrassment; now to the difference between shame and guilt. Both guilt and shame involve feeling *bad* — feeling *bad* about one's *actions* in the case of guilt; feeling *bad* about one's *self* in the experience of shame. "Picture a football field," I was once told by a well-meaning counselor, "with its two kinds of boundaries: sidelines and endlines. The sidelines are *containing* boundaries: to cross them is to 'go out of bounds,' to do something wrong. The endlines are *goal lines:* the purpose of the game is to attain them and to cross them. One feels guilty when one crosses the sideline, the restraining boundary. Feeling bad about the goal line (shame) arises not from crossing it but from *not* crossing it, from failing to attain it."

As a child, I habitually played hooky on test days: it seemed safer to do the wrong thing of skipping school than to risk falling short. The guilt of playing hooky pained less than the possible

5

shame of not measuring up on the tests. That does seem like alcoholic behavior, even without alcohol, doesn't it? In any case, in later years, I would do many similar things — *with* the help of alcohol and other chemicals.

Guilt, then, arises from an infraction, a violation or transgression of some "rule." Shame, on the contrary, occurs when a goal is not reached. Shame indicates a literal "shortcoming," a lack or defect of being. This little chart may help clarify:

	GUILT	SHAME
Results from:	a violation, a transgression, a fault of *doing* the exercise of power, of control	a failure, a falling short, a fault of *being* the lack of power, of control
Results in:	feeling of wrongdoing, sense of wickedness: "not good"	feeling of inadequacy, sense of worthlessness: "no good"

A chart is neat, but examples sometimes prove more helpful. When I cheat, or steal, I do something wrong and feel *guilt* over this violation of the rights of another. But also, on at least some occasions, my cheating or stealing can inspire *shame*. When my son got a job and worked on his own all summer to save money for college and clothes, what kind of person was I that I stole from his savings to buy booze I could hide from the family budget? Especially when it became clear that the "few dollars" I thought he'd never miss turned out to be almost half of what he had earned?

Stealing a physician's prescription pad is against the law. I knew that, but it didn't bother me much, because I had worked out a foolproof way of using those precious, powerful pieces of paper. What kind of *person* was I to do such a thing? I mean, I was acting like a junkie! Was I just a junkie? I thought up a thousand reasons why not, why I was *different,* but the nagging, gnawing thought and fear burrowed deep into my mind and never left me until I confronted that question in treatment.

Not long ago, one of my pigeons called and asked, sort of desperately, to talk with me — suggested that we go to a meeting together and then have coffee or even, since we hadn't talked lately, maybe meet for dinner before the meeting. Now, I was planning to go to that meeting, and I like Sandra. But I was hoping to go to that meeting for *my* sake. I had even thought, earlier in the day, before she called, how nice it would be to go to that small, quiet meeting — one at which I generally do not meet any of my pigeons.

Now obviously, when Sandra called I should have told her how I felt — should have admitted my own needs. But I didn't. The old alcoholic need to be perfect, the need to be thought perfect, welled up; and almost without thinking I reeled off a cock and bull story about how, despite my great fatigue and overwhelming professional obligations, I had to reach out, that very evening, to a co-worker who was obviously having trouble with booze.

Never mind Sandra's obvious disappointment (why is it that our A.A. pigeons seem to read us so well?); never mind even my rapidly drying mouth as I realized that my voice was getting higher and my words spilling out ever faster — a sure sign, for me, of dishonesty. Let's focus on the guilt and shame. Guilt: I was, in a sense, breaking a rule. Oh, there are no "rules" in A.A., but I had been taught about gratitude, and about the responsibilities of sponsorship, and besides that, I was lying. In several ways, then, according to my standards, I was doing wrong. But what nagged at me and hurt most and confused me desperately was what I had revealed about my sobriety, about *me*. Even before my hand finished replacing the telephone on its cradle, the ball of hollowness that was beginning to expand in my stomach forced me to confront my shame. Was this sobriety?

How real was my sobriety, what kind of recovering alcoholic was I, if I could so easily, glibly, almost thoughtlessly lapse into such obviously alcoholic dishonesty?

The point here, of course, is that guilt and shame are distinct: there was a difference between knowing that I had done wrong and feeling that something was wrong with me. In these examples, guilt and shame come mingled. But before we turn to examine that mingling more closely, let me finish my little story, for its end does tell something about A.A. and shame.

I called Sandra back and, without attempting an explanation, arranged to meet her and go to that meeting. Over coffee, I told her the truth: that I had lied, and how that had led me to question my own sobriety, and that she clearly had chosen a very non-perfect sponsor. Sweet Sandra! She calmed my guilt by very seriously and carefully reminding me that "there are no rules in A.A." And then, without realizing it, she spoke to and touched and soothed my shame. "I felt your rejection, and it hurt me; and even when you called back, I wasn't sure. It still hurt, and I was almost afraid you were calling back because you felt you *had* to, had to at least go through the motions. How marvelous that you're not perfect, that you are human! I wouldn't have any other kind of sponsor!" She said more, but I hugged those words close and I want to share their warmth with you now: how marvelous it is to learn, as alcoholics, that we are human — that we are not perfect, and that it is our very lack of perfection that makes us valuable to others. Experiences of shame are valuable because they teach and remind us of that very important — and very happy — reality.

It is sometimes difficult to deal with shame because experiences of shame come mixed with parallel feelings of guilt. My son's money, my doctor's prescription pad, my dishonesty with my pigeon: in each case there was guilt over wrongdoing, but concentration on that guilt would have missed the main point. I stole from my son, but I could make restitution. I broke the law, but I could stop breaking it. I lied, but I could confess the truth. However, in no case would those amends, although necessary, have been sufficient to touch and to heal my *shame* — to help me know and live with the "real me." To get sober, I had to deal with the "What kind of person?" question buried in those episodes. To stay sober, I also had to confront such questions as: "What kind of sponsor?" "What kind of sobriety?" "What kind of member of A.A.?"

Making that separation, exploring its significance, and building on its foundation are the tasks of the next chapter.

Shame and Being Human

Although guilt and shame are different, they often come mingled. Guilt, especially, rarely occurs alone. Most of the time, a wrongdoing also involves falling short or failing to live up to your ideals. When I stole, for example, I not only did wrong, I also fell short of my ideal of honesty. Although it does not always happen, one can feel shame and guilt over the same thing — the same act triggers both kinds of feeling.

When this happens, distinguishing between guilt and shame *and responding first to shame* is essential to the development and maintenance of quality sobriety. Guilt and shame are accented differently. Feelings of guilt place emphasis on the act committed: "How could I have *done that?*"

Shame, on the other hand, focuses on the person who committed the act: "How could *I* have done that? What an idiot *I* am! How *worthless* I am!"

Resolving guilt is important: that is why the Eighth and Ninth Steps play such an essential role in recovery. But confronting shame is more important because it is shame far more than guilt that lies at the root of our alcoholism. And our alcoholism itself, if we stop to think about it and have learned anything about it, involves much more a *falling short* than any sort of transgression. I denied my alcoholism for so long, not because alcoholism was a bad thing, but because admitting that I was an alcoholic would have meant acknowledging that I was a bad person.

The first truth that A.A. teaches us concerns the reality of our personal limitation: "We admitted we were powerless over alcohol — that our lives had become unmanageable." The first thing we learn in Alcoholics Anonymous (and how welcome a lesson it is!) is that A.A. is concerned not with the thing, alcoholism, but with the person, the alcoholic. A.A. thus speaks to and touches our shame in its very First Step. The acknowledgment "I am an alcoholic" contained in the admission "powerless over alcohol" invites us and *frees* us to accept the truth of our essential limitation. Newcomers to Alcoholics Anonymous thus come to admit, to accept, and even to embrace essential limitation as the *definition* of their alcoholic (human) condition.

The acceptance of essential limitation is the core and the heart of Alcoholics Anonymous. This acceptance, indeed, becomes both the price and the reward of our First Step admission: "powerless over alcohol." By this emphasis on essential limitation, Alcoholics Anonymous teaches us a profound and healing truth: accepting the reality of self-as-feared is necessary to finding the reality of self-as-is. Learning this truth enables us to begin on the road to sobriety. Building upon it becomes, in sobriety, equally necessary to progress and grow.

As we grow in sobriety, we must remember this first lesson; but if we truly *grow* in sobriety, we also come to see that our alcoholism is not our only essential limitation. We learn, within Alcoholics Anonymous, that our fundamental limitation is not that we are alcoholic, but that we are *human.*

Alcoholics Anonymous as a way of life builds on our alcoholism to teach us that to be human is to be essentially limited. We exist in a contradiction, between opposite pulls to be more-than-human and to be less-than-human. The idea should be amply familiar to us from our days of active alcoholism. We drank, often, in an effort to be *more* than we were: more witty, more relaxed, more charming, more *whatever.* And the result of that effort, once we became alcoholics, was inevitably the opposite: we got sick, or passed out, or made fools of ourselves, or in any of far too many ways concluded our drinking far *less* than the human beings we were before we turned to alcohol.

At other times, perhaps, we drank in the effort to be "less-than-human": we drank to be less inhibited, less awake, less feeling, less aware. The result of those efforts was inevitably to heighten the sensibilities we had hoped to diminish, wasn't it? We perhaps shed an inhibition, but we became acutely sensitive to imagined insults. Or we found ourselves less sleepy than ever, aware of even the slightest sound. Often, the pain we tried to escape became intensified by the very drugs we took seeking relief. Remember when?

Blaise Pascal said, "He who would be an angel becomes a beast."[3] The attempt to be more than human leads to being less than human. Another thinker, George Santayana, suggested a related observation: "It is necessary to become a beast if one is ever to be a spirit."[4] That is, in order to know the heights of human existence, one must also touch its depths.

Together, these understandings summarize the heart of what Alcoholics Anonymous teaches us about being human — about

13

being "a god who shits."[5] In the A.A. diagnosis, active alcoholics drink in the attempt to be *either* an angel *or* a beast. Sobriety means accepting the reality that we are *both*. Acceptance of this reality of being human comes easily to the alcoholic who understands alcoholism, because the condition of alcoholism mirrors the *essence* of the human condition.

Shame and the Non-moral

(Love, Sickness, Freedom and Reality)

Three characteristics of shame help us come to terms with its painfulness: 1) shame can arise over a *non-moral* failing; 2) it tends to be occasioned by an *involuntary* shortcoming; 3) it seems magnified by the very *triviality* of its stimulus. These qualities aid in distinguishing shame from guilt and shed light on the nature of the essential limitation that Alcoholics Anonymous teaches us lies at the core of the human condition.

Guilt, you may recall from our earlier discussion, arises from the violation of some restraining boundary. This implies that guilt characteristically has to do with moral transgression, results from a voluntary act, and tends to be proportionate to the seriousness of the offense committed. Guilt thus follows from a wrong that one chooses to do; and the graver the wrong, the greater the guilt.

Shame differs from guilt on all three counts, even when both arise together after a wrongdoing that marks also a falling short. We will come to understand shame best, however, by separating these qualities that characterize it and by examining cases of shame uncontaminated by guilt. The next two chapters will examine shame's connection with the involuntary and the trivial.

Although shame may arise over a moral lapse such as stealing, some of our failings have nothing to do with morality. Two such cases seem especially important for us to deal with as alcoholics: failure in love and the failure of sickness.

Love

Perhaps the most common source of non-moral shame, and not only for alcoholics, is disappointment in love. But especially for alcoholics, such shame can be particularly dangerous. How many times have we turned to alcohol out of the frustration of feeling unloved or rejected? Guilt over wrongdoing plays no role in such cases; we seek rather the solace of the bottle in the attempt somehow to warm or to fill the chill, hollow emptiness of felt inadequacy.

Defeat, disappointment, frustration, or failure evoke shame. Guilt, as transgression, always involves aggression: one feels guilty about the aggression. Shame arises over the failure — or the foolishness — of the attempt, rather than over the attempt itself.

Shame arising from failure in love can haunt the alcoholic drinking or sober. Being "passed over," failing to win a hoped for and sought after raise or promotion, can wound painfully. Defeat and disappointment, frustration and failure, haunt the *human* condition. As active alcoholics, our disadvantage on such occasions was that we had a cop-out that inevitably made things worse. Our advantage as recovering alcoholics is that we know what it is to be human, and we have learned to find solace even in our hurt, for that hurt proves that we are human, whereas once we very nearly were not.

Sickness

Painful as is the shame of failure in love, the failure of sickness can be worse. To be ill is not to transgress, to *do* wrong, but to fall short, to *be* lacking. Health is the norm: we naturally feel that we should be healthy. Lacking health, we feel that there is something wrong not only with us, but about us. Being sick implies inadequacy.

We need to think about that, for both the disease concept of alcoholism and A.A.'s emphasis on alcoholism as malady serve two functions. They remove alcoholism from the category of morality and thus render us less guilty; but they also firmly locate us as alcoholics in the shameful situation of being chronically ill. Alcoholics Anonymous, in emphasizing that alcoholism is malady rather than sin, also proclaims that there is a difference between the guilt feeling of wickedness and the shamed sense of worthlessness. A.A.'s experience — *our* experience — teaches clearly that the alcoholic's problem is not that he is wicked, but that he feels worthless.

The feeling of worthlessness is worse than the sense of wickedness. How, then, does it mark progress in therapy to label alcoholism a disease? Does it not rather render the plight of us poor alcoholics even more pitiful and hopeless, if it means exchanging guilt for shame? It might seem so, except that the experience of over a million members of Alcoholics Anonymous clearly testifies that "It Works!"

17

Freedom and reality

It works because it teaches reality, and the first truth of human reality is that we are limited. Alcoholics Anonymous understands the deep danger to sobriety of the alcoholic's tendency to demand "all-or-nothing." A.A. therefore teaches us, as recovering alcoholics, not only the *fact* of our limitation and our *need* to accept it, but also the positive side of that limitation and its acceptance. There is an equation — a necessary connection — between being limited and being real. We see this most clearly in the matter of *freedom*.

The drinking alcoholic turned to alcohol in search of freedom; the recovering alcoholic searches for freedom from alcohol. The experience of Alcoholics Anonymous teaches us that the second search will prove as vain as the first, unless we accept the simple truth that to be human is to be *both* free and unfree. For the alcoholic, as for any other human being, there is no absolute freedom.

As recovering alcoholics, we learn first in Alcoholics Anonymous that our freedom, *although* real, is limited. Conversely our freedom, *although* limited, is real. To attain the freedom to not-drink, we accept limitation of our freedom to drink. In recovery we must come to see that this acceptance is not a concession. The word "although," must be replaced in our thinking by the affirmation "because": *because* real, our freedom is limited; *because* limited, our freedom is real.

A.A. experience continually reminds us, as recovering alcoholics, how the apparently unlimited freedom to drink inevitably leads to increasing bondage and ever greater losses of freedom. Some of us, in defending our "freedom" and "right" to drink, lost jobs and status, wealth and love and more; some, we know, lost life itself. The same A.A. experience progressively reveals, on the other hand, how the limited freedom to not-drink brings in its wake *ever-increasing freedom.*

As recovering alcoholics within Alcoholics Anonymous, we thus learn a profound truth: with freedom, as with any other human phenomenon, to be real is to be limited, for limitation *proves* reality. This understanding enables both joyous acceptance of the human condition and true recovery from alcoholism. It enables both because that acceptance and recovery are one and the same.

Shame and the Involuntary

(Problems of Willing)

Guilt implies choice. Shame, on the other hand, occurs over something involuntary: it arises from *incapacity,* from the *failure* of choice. The memories of car accidents, of tumbles down stairs, of food or drink spilled on friends or guests, remain painful well into sobriety. Of course we didn't "choose" to do those things — they were clearly involuntary, but can't those memories still sting?

The pain in shame arises from the failure of choice, of will, of *self.* A married man who committed adultery might feel both guilt and shame: guilt over the violation of the marriage promise; shame at falling short of the marriage ideal. The man who finds himself sexually impotent with a woman he loves will feel predominantly shame: the question of morality does not enter, and surely such sexual disability is anything but voluntary.

When a drinking alcoholic asks "Why?" — "Why do I drink; I know I don't want to!" any sober alcoholic who knows and lives the philosophy of Alcoholics Anonymous knows better than to try to prove that he really did want to. The A.A. answer accepts involuntariness: "You didn't want to, but you did. You did because you are an alcoholic. That is what an alcoholic is: one who drinks when he doesn't want to. The answer to 'Why?' lies not in your will, in its strength or its weakness, but in the fact that you are alcoholic."

The involuntariness of shame is important because we learn from it something about the human will and its limitations. The alcoholic cannot will to not-drink any more than the insomniac can will to fall asleep. The example is exact: in each case, we can will the means, the context that will enable the desired end to come about; but also in both cases, any attempt directly to will the end — any effort to seize the object desired — proves self-defeating.

There are two very different ways in which we attain two different kinds of things that we will. In some matters, we choose particular objects: I can choose right now whether to write in pencil or with pen, whether to keep writing, or to refill my coffee cup, or to go for a walk. In other matters, we choose an orientation, a direction, a context that will allow — we hope — our end to be achieved. I choose right now to sit at this desk, with good light and away from distractions, and to rehearse in my mind the many things I have learned at meetings of Alcoholics Anonymous. But I cannot will, as I will to use this pen, either brilliant thoughts or that you — one particular reader — understand my point here. Indeed, were I to attempt to will either, the writing would cease, for the very effort would overwhelm me and become a "block."

We get into trouble with willing when we try to will directions, contexts, in the same way that we will to choose objects. There are some contexts that vanish under such attempts at coercion. I cannot will sobriety, but I can choose not to pick up the first drink, today. I cannot, over any length of time, will to not-drink; but I can choose to go to A.A. meetings and to work on the Steps of the A.A. program. If I should try to will sobriety in the same way that I choose to pick up the telephone to call my sponsor, I would be drunk within a week. If I should try to will to not-drink in the same way that I choose to get in my car to go to an A.A. meeting, my track record before finding Alcoholics Anonymous offers ample proof that I'd be getting in my car to go out to buy booze.

And all this is true not only of things having to do with drinking and sobriety. I can, right now, will to write vividly, but not directly that you continue to read. I can will knowledge, but not wisdom; submission, but not humility; self-assertion, but not courage; physical nearness, but not emotional closeness.

Because shame so often arises from the failure of the effort to will what cannot be willed, experiences of shame contain an important lesson for us as alcoholics. To know shame is to realize that certain things fall outside the reach of what we often think of as "will," beyond the scope of the manipulative will that chooses objects. Sobriety, wisdom, humility, courage and love are not objects: we can choose to move toward them, but any effort to seize them runs the self-defeating risk of destroying them. Again, recall the promise of Alcoholics Anonymous; "progress rather than perfection" — movement toward rather than absolute possession.

To be human is to be limited, and because our human will is especially limited, there can be no absolutes or unlimitednesses within our human power. Alcoholics Anonymous inculcates this truth by clearly directing our attention to the two areas in which the alcoholic seeks, by using alcohol, to deny the limitation of the will. These two areas are control and dependence.

Limited control

Drinking alcoholics, we learn if we listen carefully at meetings of Alcoholics Anonymous, drink alcohol in an effort to achieve control — *absolute* control — over their feelings and their environment. Whether we drink to feel "high" or to relax, to make us witty or to soothe our pain, we drink to control. In drinking to control mood, we attempt to deny that our moods depend upon situations — and especially upon people — outside ourselves, beyond our control. We drink in an effort to deny such dependence; yet, in this effort, our dependence upon alcohol itself becomes absolute.

The alcoholic's problem, then, involves the demand for unlimited control and the denial of real dependence. The fellowship and program of Alcoholics Anonymous meet this double problem in a twofold way. First, A.A. confronts us as alcoholics with the plain facts that, so far as alcohol itself is concerned, we are absolutely out of control and absolutely dependent. Then, after we accept this reality by the admission "powerless over alcohol," Alcoholics Anonymous both pre-scribes and teaches the exercise of *limited* control and *limited* dependence.

The Seventh Step of the A.A. program originally began with the words, "Humbly on our knees. . ." Kneeling is a middle position — halfway between standing upright and lying flat. In a sense, Alcoholics Anonymous understands the alcoholic to be someone who, by claiming absolute control and denying all dependence, insists on trying to stand upright unaided, only to fall repeatedly flat on his face — often literally in the gutter. To the alcoholic lying prone, A.A. suggests: "Get *up* on your knees — you can do something, but not everything." Later, as we

24

progress toward sobriety, A.A. often has occasion to temper our tendencies to grandiosity with a similar suggestion: "Get *down* on your knees — you can do something, but not everything."

A.A.'s emphasis on limited control runs through its whole program. Think about that encouragement combined with the admonition, "You can do something, but not everything." We are warned against promising "never to drink again" and taught instead how not to take the *first* drink, "one day at a time." We learn to reach for the telephone instead of the bottle. A.A. encourages us to attend meetings, something we can do, rather than to avoid all contact with alcohol, which is virtually impossible. For me, the whole point of limited control is beautifully summed up by the Serenity Prayer: "Grant me the serenity to accept the things I cannot change, the courage to change the things I can, and the wisdom to know the difference."

The "can" and "cannot" of the Serenity Prayer remind me powerfully not only of the limitations on my ability to control, but also of how as recovering alcoholics we owe our priceless possession of freedom to the fellowship and program of Alcoholics Anonymous. As we learn in A.A., alcoholism is an obsessive-compulsive malady: the active alcoholic is one who *must* drink, who *cannot* not-drink. Thus, when we join A.A., we do not surrender any "freedom to drink": rather we gain the freedom to not-drink. I sometimes think, indeed, that within Alcoholics Anonymous our passage from "mere dryness" to "true sobriety" is marked precisely by that change of perception. We begin, as each of us must, by "putting the cork in the bottle." We start by accepting the prohibition, "I cannot drink." But somewhere along the line, if we work the Steps and live our program, we come to see that that acceptance is not primarily a prohibition, a negative. Our life in recovery discovers the joyous affirmation behind that apparent restraint, and we begin to rejoice in this happy new reality — in the *real* freedom of "I *can* not-drink."

Limited dependence

This understanding of human freedom suggests not only "limited control," but also "limited dependence." The dead-end trap in which active alcoholics are mired consists of *two* denials: their denial of dependence upon alcohol is but one manifestation of their larger denial of dependence upon *anything* outside themselves. Alcoholics turn to alcohol *inside* themselves in order to enforce that denial of dependence.

In confronting this dual denial, Alcoholics Anonymous subtly challenges a frequent modern assumption. Other therapies tend to approach alcoholics from their own point of view — to agree that all dependence, but especially *essential* dependence such as that which binds alcoholics to their chemical, is humiliating and dehumanizing. They try to convince the alcoholic that maturity and "recovery" — becoming fully human — mean overcoming all such dependencies. Diagnosing alcoholism, virtually all modern therapies see the alcoholic's problem as "dependence on alcohol," and they endeavor to break the alcoholic's dependence.

The larger-wisdomed insight of Alcoholics Anonymous does not exactly contradict this understanding. Indeed, A.A. agrees with and accepts this diagnosis that the alcoholic's problem is "dependence on alcohol." But Alcoholics Anonymous penetrates deeper, locating the definition's deeper truth by shifting its implicit emphasis. A.A. interprets the experience of its members — *our* experience — as revealing that the alcoholic's problem is not "*dependence* on alcohol," but "dependence on *alcohol.*" To be human *is* to be limited, Alcoholics Anonymous insists, and therefore to be dependent. The alcoholic's choice — the *human* choice — lies not between dependence and independence, but

26

between that upon which one will acknowledge dependence: a less than human substance such as alcohol within oneself, or a more than individual reality that remains essentially outside — beyond — the self.

Shame and the Trivial

(The Exposure of Denial)

The third and final characteristic of shame to be examined is the frequent triviality of its source — the apparent disproportion in shame that makes it literally such a monstrous experience. Usually, when we feel guilt, the intensity of our guilt is proportionate to the gravity of our offense: the more serious the transgression, the greater the guilt.

Shame, on the contrary, tends to be triggered by the most trivial of failings, by some small and even picayune detail. This happens because such little things point unmistakably to the failure of self *as self,* rather than as breaker of some rule. The employee who embezzled a thousand dollars, when he comes to doing his Eighth and Ninth Steps, feels mostly guilt. The person who has cadged quarters off a co-worker's desk or consistently ignored the office coffee pot's plea for coin contributions, feels more shame than guilt. If we can tap that shame, can touch that triviality, we will find in A.A.'s Eighth and Ninth Steps profound help in confronting ourselves as we are. Attending to the trivial invites examining "What kind of *person* am I to have done that?" The more trivial the "that," the greater the light shed upon "person."

The disproportion inherent in experiences of shame — the tendency of shame to be greater as its apparent occasion is smaller — also reveals something about the appropriateness of Alcoholics Anonymous as a therapy for shame. In a sense, shame is addictive. The disproportion in the shame reaction tends to magnify shame itself: we become ashamed at the very inappropriateness of our reaction, and therefore ashamed of shame itself. Shame becomes, in a way, insatiable: the more we feel it, the more we feel it — a vicious circle not unlike the squirrel cage that is alcoholism. Perhaps because of this parallel, it is this characteristic of shame — the apparent triviality of its occasion — that I found it most helpful to fasten on, as I progressed in sobriety, in trying to turn experiences of shame to constructive use. Let me try to explain why and perhaps also to show how.

Alcoholics Anonymous teaches us to locate the "root of our troubles" in the selfishness of "self-centeredness" — in *pride*. As drinking alcoholics, we think ourselves exceptional, special, *different*, and this tendency does not suddenly cease in early sobriety. This is one reason why we hear so often at A.A. meetings the advice: "Identify, Don't Compare." That is, concentrate on how you are *like* us, not on how you think you are different. Despite that frequently repeated warning, however, most of us go through a stage, in early recovery, in which our enthusiasm for A.A. and for the very newness of the experience of honesty tempts us to judge and proclaim our-selves, as we review our personal history of alcoholism, *especially* "wicked."

I cannot claim to have completely escaped that trap in my own early sobriety, but something I heard in treatment helped me at least avoid becoming mired in it. A speaker told us that for *both* drinking and sober alcoholics: "The alcoholic's problem is not that he feels, 'I am a worm'; nor even that he feels, 'I am very special.' The alcoholic's main problem is that he feels, 'I am a very special worm.' "

That insight has helped me in many ways. At times, I'm sure you've noticed, even "good" A.A. meetings seem momentarily to be in danger of degenerating into "Can you top this?" competitions. When that begins to happen (and I must admit that at times I catch myself contributing to it) remembering "very special worm" helps to rescue me, and often the meeting. After all, our telling of stories at A.A. meetings is related to (although not the same as) the Fifth Step of the A.A. program. They are most alike, indeed, in providing therapy for precisely the "very special worm" snare.

"Admitted to God, to ourselves, and to another human being, the exact nature of our wrongs." Such confession is, of course, an ancient religious practice as well as a modern therapeutic technique. But Alcoholics Anonymous took it over directly from the Oxford Group within which A.A. was born, and the Group used the public confession of "sharing" specifically to minister to its adherents' shame rather than their guilt. As one of the Oxford Group books used by the early A.A. members says: "This sharing leads to the discovery that sins we thought were so bad are quite run-of-the-mill. The regard of one's sins as particularly awful is a vicious form of pride that is overcome by sharing."[6]

The A.A. practice of story-telling at meetings, like the more private Fifth Step , serves the same function: to drive home the point that the alcoholic is very ordinary. I suspect this is why Bill Wilson, in writing about A.A.'s Fifth Step in *Twelve Steps and Twelve Traditions,* presented it as ending "the old pangs of anxious apartness" and beginning the alcoholic's "emergence from isolation."

Exposure

Because shame's stimulus is so often trivial, shame itself frequently catches us by surprise. This helps to make experiences of shame episodes of exposure. Experiences of shame throw a flooding and searching light on what and who we are, painfully uncovering unrecognized aspects of personality. Exposure to oneself lies at the heart of shame: we discover, in experiences of shame, the most sensitive, intimate, and vulnerable parts of our *self.*

Somerset Maugham, in his study *Of Human Bondage,* acutely penetrates the essence of shame as the exposure of one's own weakness. The story describes a boy, Philip, away from home for the first time, at school. Philip has a clubfoot, and his new classmates tease him, demanding to see his deformity. Although he wants their friendship, Philip refuses to show the other boys his deformed foot. One night, however, a group of the boys attack Philip in the dormitory, after he has gone to bed. The school bully twists his arm until Philip sticks his leg out of the bed, allowing them all to stare at his misshapen foot. After a moment of laughter, the boys run off. And Philip?

> Philip . . . got his teeth in the pillow so that his sobbing should be inaudible. He was not crying for the pain they had caused him, nor for the humiliation he had suffered when they looked at his foot, but with rage at himself because, unable to stand the torture, he had put out his foot of his own accord.[7]

Exposure of his deformity to others was less painful to Philip than the exposure to himself of his own weakness.

Alcoholism — in fact, any chemical dependency — often arises from and is almost always connected with the effort to conceal weakness, to prevent its exposure *to oneself.* The alcoholic or addict uses a chemical in order to *hide,* and especially to hide from self. The attempt at hiding reveals that the critical problem underlying such behavior is *shame.*

This is one reason why distinguishing between shame and guilt is so important. It is also a large reason why the more classic therapies, or the usual consolations of religion, provide little help to the alcoholic. During the years I was drinking, wanting to be absolved of guilt was *not* my major problem. If anything, I was pleading dimly but passionately within myself *to be able to feel guilty.* At some deep level I knew, even as an active alcoholic, that others' admonitions to "mend my ways" or even marshalling my own will to "grow up" didn't work. But I sought out such admonitions, at times, from therapists and clergy, and I at least went through the motions of such willing.

Yet, more deeply, I somehow realized, even as I did all this, that I had to maintain my addictions. What I didn't realize, then, was that I had to in order to conceal my unendurable shame from myself. Of the other therapies I tried — or pretended to try — many, *couldn't* work, because I could not afford to allow any interference with my true problem of chemical dependency. Any such interference seemed to threaten my very being, and so I sought help only from those who I knew — or hoped — would not interfere with it.

Let me tell you — or remind you — of something that we all know now, as recovering alcoholics, but refused to face then, as active alcoholics: a major component of alcoholic addiction is the attempt to avoid or to deny *pain.* The *real* pain that we try primarily to deny, let me suggest, is the existential pain of shame: the gnawing hollowness of the fearful feeling that in some essential way we are failures as human beings.

Denial and hiding

We thus again see the wisdom of the "treatment" provided by Alcoholics Anonymous, which aims and claims not to cure our alcoholism, but to care for us as alcoholics. Because it realizes that *shame* is the root of our alcoholism, A.A. sets out directly to touch that sore nerve, to enable us to confront our own shame. A.A. does this by allowing — and at times even by bringing about — the humiliation that we had sought so desperately to avoid by our use of chemicals. The process, which we will explore at depth in the next three chapters, is amazingly simple. It is precisely our falling short, our shame as alcoholics, that becomes the source of our new sober life in A.A. We come to see, in Alcoholics Anonymous, that our most meaningful strengths flow directly from our most shameful weakness.

It is fascinating to observe how Alcoholics Anonymous cuts through our last vestiges of prideful denial and taps our humiliation and shame. We see it most clearly with beginners, although groups will apply the same treatment to oldtimers. Perhaps because I sought help from so many other places before Alcoholics Anonymous, I cherish an image that I think aptly sums up the essence of A.A.'s initial approach to our shame.

Any hurting person who seeks help brings to therapy a tiny, flickering flame of self-respect. Classic, guilt-oriented therapies strive to nourish that tiny glimmer, to enlarge self-respect. The initial response of Alcoholics Anonymous is different. Newcomers who display self-respect meet with caring confrontation: they are offered, for example, a carefully half-filled cup of coffee. Such confrontation of lingering denial invites hesitant newcomers to acknowledge the fact of their shakes and to realize that the coffee-server who recognizes the shakes accepts them. The message is less "It's okay" than "It's tough, but I've been there too." More stubborn cases may, in time, be told: "Take the cotton out of your ears and put it in your mouth!" Any flicker of self-respect that reveals denial of the felt worthlessness of shame is gently quashed rather than nourished within A.A. Why? Because A.A. experience testifies that, until that denial is shattered, its own constructive therapy cannot be effective. The alcoholic must confront self-as-feared to find the reality of self-as-is.

Denial is the characteristic defense of alcoholics. Against denial, the shared honesty of mutual vulnerability openly acknowledged operates most effectively. Denial involves the *hiding* of felt inadequacy of being. Shame, as herein explained, relates so intimately to denial because it results not merely from a sense of failure, but from a sense of *essential* failure — failure *as a human being*, the failure of *existence*. This understanding captures, I believe, the insight of Dr. Harry Tiebout, who was Bill Wilson's own therapist and whose writings help so many of us understand both our alcoholism and our recovery. Tiebout's greatest contribution was his distinction between "compliance," which he saw as worse than useless because it obscured the obsessive-compulsive nature of alcoholism; and "surrender," which he presented as the key to the process of recovery. Tiebout's compliance may be understood as motivated by guilt; surrender, as enabled by the alcoholic's acceptance of shame.

Denial, Tiebout realized, could continue despite acknowledgment of guilt — despite, indeed, attempts to make amends for guilt. Guilt, he suggested, could even be a defense against confronting and accepting what is denied. For example, when an alcoholic accepts responsibility for what he or she did while drinking as preferable to admitting that the drinking itself was out of control, then guilt is a form of denial. That was a trick I often played on my unwary therapists, some of whom fell into the trap of praising my "maturity" and "responsibility" and my "taking charge" of my own life. Ha! Real guilt fears punishment and tries to escape it. The person whose problem is shame, on the other hand, tends to seek and even to embrace punishment. Admitting "guilt," and paying for it, confirms the denial of what is most deeply feared and most profoundly painful — the sense of having failed as a human being. How sweet it was to be praised for my "honesty" at the very moment that I was being most dishonest, to be commended for my "courage" at the very moment that I was being most cowardly! *Sweet?!*

My alcoholic and chemical history was one long tale of ever-increasing denial and hiding. I hid from others and from myself. I denied not only my alcoholism and chemical dependency, but ever larger areas of my life and realities about myself. I tried to pull over myself that chemical veil, to deny reality by hiding behind alcohol and pills, until one day it seemed that there was nothing left to hide. Not "nothing else" — *nothing at all.*

At that hollow, empty moment, moved by the love of two A.A. members, a clergyman and a cop, I reached out for treatment and for Alcoholics Anonymous. Abandoning my denial and hiding and beginning to find my real self was not easy. I remember vividly an incident in treatment: a group session after we had somewhat begun to know each other and the principles of A.A. I forget exactly what I was talking about; but I do recall that I was trying so hard to be honest, yet sensing within myself and from the glances of the group that somehow my denial was still clinging to me, and I to it.

My words trailed off into silence. Finally, one of the group members, a young counselor-trainee, looked at me sadly and spoke gently in words of pained love: "If you — *all* of you — were ever on that TV show where they said, 'Would the *real you* please stand up!' . . . you wouldn't know what to do, which one of you should stand up, would you?"

The blinding accuracy of those words cut, but the love and concern and identification that I heard in them — and in the empathetic, understanding nods of the others in the group — began to heal. On occasion, as I progress in sobriety, I re-live that scene in my imagination. A few times, when I have felt the need for help with my continuing denials and fearful hidings, I have re-told the story at my A.A. discussion group. Each time, I have been healed further.

Recovering alcoholics know the treacheries of denial and hiding. And we learn, from the wisdom of A.A., to tap the trivial instances that expose our shame. That exposure, within A.A., allows and invites us to move beyond our alcoholic denials and hidings. Exploring how this happens and why it works is the task we turn to in the next chapters.

Part II:

Coping with Shame

Needing Others

Growth in sobriety may be understood as the continuing process by which we get beyond our hiding, transcend our denial, solve our shame. How do we achieve this? Alcoholics Anonymous provides a *model* and suggests a *method* of attaining continuing growth. The *model* is A.A.'s penetration of our denial that we are alcoholics. The *method* is A.A.'s inculcation of the reality that as limited — alcoholic — human beings, we need other people. Other people are not the problem in shame, but the solution. Denial and shame have to do with our limitations. We deny our need for alcohol and other people because admitting our need forces us to face our limitations. We hide our limitations because we are ashamed of them.

Early in my alcoholic career, I denied to myself as well as

to others that I was seeking comfort or excitement in alcohol because other *people* could not fill my insatiable needs. At parties, for example, "a few drinks" and a strategic location near the liquor supply became far more important to the "success" of the evening than any people I might meet. Alcohol more and more furnished a surer source of satisfaction than "all that silly party conversation." A bit further down the road of alcoholism I shifted more directly to denying any need for others: "Just let me alone — I can lick this thing by myself."

Alcoholics Anonymous worked — and works — for me because its fellowship and program continually break through these twin denials of my need for alcohol and my need for others. A.A. as a fellowship helped me discover and admit my need for others by being the one place — the *only* place by the time I got there — where I myself was needed, and *needed precisely and only as an alcoholic.* Realizing that enabled me to admit that I was an "alcoholic" and, therefore, to admit my insatiable need for alcohol. As a program, A.A. builds on my acceptance of myself as an alcoholic and an ever deepening awareness of my need for others. Without those others in A.A., I could never have admitted my own alcoholism. And I fairly soon came to realize that the "We" that begins the First of A.A.'s Twelve Steps stands also at the beginning of the other eleven.

Outsiders who study Alcoholics Anonymous usually recognize and often even fasten on our twin admissions of need — for alcohol and for other alcoholics. Many of the supposedly smart ones look down upon us because of these admissions: they try to explain away our recovery according to "labeling" or "deviant role" theories; or they interpret A.A. away as "the substituting of a social dependence for a drug dependence," or as "accepting the emotional immaturity of alcoholics and supplying a crutch for it." We know better, I think, and we do not need outside support — although there happens to be plenty of that, and also from some pretty respectable "smart" people — to validate the joyous reality of a human life, humanly lived, to which our own lives and the stories of over a million sober members of Alcoholics Anonymous attest.

In dealing with shame, as I have tried to suggest, other people are not the problem, but the solution. The experience of Alcoholics Anonymous teaches us further that, for "others" to be shame's solution, they cannot be *merely* "others" — merely, that is, objects. Within A.A. we do not relate to each other "objectively." Objectivity is a quality that is valued in the medical — the curing — model. Think, for example, of the surgeon. Surgeons do not operate on their own family members, on persons with whom they have a *caring* relationship. Further, even the ordinary patient's body is so prepared and draped for surgery that his or her personhood and individuality are concealed insofar as possible. Everything about the ritual and procedures of the operating room is designed to enable surgeons to perform their skills upon a body rather than upon a person.

But Alcoholics Anonymous is not medicine nor surgery. In fact, one thing the early A.A. members found most objectionable about the Oxford Group was its use of the term "soul-surgery." That first generation of Alcoholics Anonymous sensed that wasn't how *they* worked, how A.A. worked. The uniqueness of Alcoholics Anonymous was that it did not claim to cure, but to *care*. In A.A., therefore, "others" are not *objects* who are "out there." "Identify, Don't Compare" mandates getting inside of and being with, as opposed precisely to standing off or viewing "objectively."

Accepting persons *as persons,* as fellow subjects rather than as mere objects, is the key to the A.A. model of *caring* rather than curing. This caring model pioneered by and lived out within Alcoholics Anonymous presents fully *human* relationships as characterized by two qualities: complementarity and mutuality.

43

"Complementarity" means the acceptance that individuals *fit into* each other, thus fulfilling each other rather than diminishing self or other. In such relationships, each is to each other according to the needs of *both*. "Mutuality" underlines the back-and-forth-ness in this: the two-way, reciprocal nature of human relationships that are truly human.

What does this mean in practice? Members of Alcoholics Anonymous achieve this complementarity and mutuality — this relationship of fitting into and fulfilling each other — because they know that they need each other *as alcoholics*. I, as an alcoholic, need you, as an alcoholic. This is why, at A.A. meetings, we proclaim "I am an alcoholic" as a joyous affirmation of positive identity rather than as some grudging complaint or concession that is to be regretted. Because "I am an alcoholic," I need you; because you are also an alcoholic, my need fits into your need rather than threatening to overwhelm you. I hear a similar message when you identify yourself as alcoholic: because you are an alcoholic, you need me, and your need enhances rather than threatens my existence, for I too am an alcoholic. Because we are alcoholics, and therefore essentially limited, our needs for each other are also essentially limited. The first thing that we know about each other is that we need *each other;* thus the foundation for mutuality is established.

In the three brief chapters that follow, we turn to examine each of the three mutualities that the fellowship and program of Alcoholics Anonymous teach and enable — the three ways of living out our human need for others that help keep us sober as A.A. members. They help us keep sober because they help us be *real.* They allow and encourage us to be the kind of human beings who find meaning in living with others rather than seeking the lonely destruction of chemicals. Learning the reality *about* our need for others invites us to embrace the reality *of* that need for others.

Making a Difference

Finding and accepting *mutuality* is essential to the sobriety that solves shame. The discovery and living out of mutuality enables us to transcend the "self-centeredness" that Alcoholics Anonymous teaches us is "the root of our troubles." The first and probably the most important mutuality that we find and learn how to put into practice in A.A. involves *making a difference*. Here, most clearly, all the history and experience of Alcoholics Anonymous teaches us the profound truth that underlies the very concept of mutuality: we get by giving; we give by getting.

The ability to make a difference is a deeply vital human need. In a way, in fact, Alcoholics Anonymous came into being because it recognized and met this basic need of even the "hopeless" alcoholic. For six months after he himself attained sobriety in November, 1934, Bill Wilson failed in all his attempts to help other alcoholics: none of them wanted what Bill thought he had to give. But on Mothers' Day of 1935, when Bill found himself stuck in Akron, Ohio and became desperately afraid that he would drink again, he sought out Doctor Bob Smith for what Bob, as an alcoholic, *could give him.* Bill sought out Bob not to give, but to get: because of this, his attempts to give finally became effective. Doctor Bob listened and was touched, because Bill not only admitted his own need for him, but even *thanked* Bob for listening, and for thus helping him — Bill — to stay sober.

Perhaps an even clearer and more significant moment occurred at the bedside of the alcoholic who was to become "A.A. Number Three." Wilson and Smith told Bill D., when they called on him in the hospital, that talking with him was the only way *they* could stay sober. Bill D. believed them and *therefore* — as he tells us in his own story — he listened.

> All the other people that had talked to me wanted to help *me*, and my pride prevented me from listening to them, and caused only resentment on my part, but I felt as if I would be a real stinker if I did not listen to a couple of fellows for a short time, if that would cure *them.*[8]

Do you see the point — the first "secret" of A.A.? Somewhere in the world, at this very moment, two A.A. members are finishing up with an obviously "hopeless" Twelfth Step call. They have each told their stories to the bleary-eyed, swaying drunk who popped down "one or two more for courage" after calling the A.A. number, and they are wondering whether this sorry hunk of humanity, besotted with booze and self-pity, even heard anything they have said. Clearly, they can do nothing more today; but as they stand up to leave, one of the callers remembers what makes a "successful" Twelfth Step call and blurts out in honest gratitude: "You've got our phone numbers, and I hope you'll call when you're feeling better. I don't think we've helped you much today, in the condition you're in, but I want to thank you for helping me. Seeing you like this, and telling you my story, helps me keep sober today. I know that I'm not going to take a drink today, and I thank you for giving me that gift and this opportunity."

And somehow, perhaps, *that* message gets through the alcoholic's self-pitying haze of self-hatred. That honest "thank you" somehow taps the desperation that motivated the call to A.A. It touches and soothes the absolute sense of "no good" that eats away at the alcoholic's last shred of self-respect. Whatever else is said as the Twelfth Steppers leave, the alcoholic knows that something has changed, something is now different. There is a place, there are people to whom the alcoholic has something of value to give.

Every human being *needs* to make a difference. Alcoholics Anonymous recognizes and utilizes this reality, and thus its wisdom taps an unchanging truth of the human condition. To be human is to require "significance" — *place* in another person's world.

> It seems to be a universal human desire to wish to occupy a place in the world of at least one other person. Perhaps the greatest solace in religion is the sense that one lives in the Presence of an Other.[9]
>
> * * * *
>
> We ourselves want to be needed. We do not only have needs, we are also strongly motivated by neededness. . . We are restless when we are not needed, because we feel "unfinished," "incomplete," and we can only get completed in and through these relationships. We are motivated to search not only for what we lack and need but also for that for which we are needed, what is wanted from us.[10]

We introduced, in the preceding chapter, the terms "mutuality" and "complementarity." Mutuality implies having significance, making a difference, by *both* giving and getting. Complementarity means that one both gets *by* giving and *by* getting. Alcoholics Anonymous not only teaches these truths — it enables even the most "hopeless" drunk to live them out, and by living them out to attain the honorable condition of alcoholic. When we say at A.A. meetings, "I am an alcoholic," we proclaim not only that we need, but that even from the depths of our need, we have something to *give*.

We learn, as recovering alcoholics, that we need. By accepting our need, we confront our shame. But one of our deepest needs, we discover, contains shame's solution — *if* there are others like us. The need to be needed is the solution for our shame. The need to be needed gnaws sharply. If shame is to be resolved, we need to be needed *for our very need*. To find this need met is to put shame itself to shame.

Honesty with Self and with Others

The second mutuality that we learn and live within Alcoholics Anonymous involves honesty. A.A. experience vividly teaches that there is an essential connection of mutuality between honesty with self and honesty with others. Most alcoholics who reach Alcoholics Anonymous already know quite a bit about the necessary mutuality between honesty with self and with others. Our drinking experience before reaching A.A. was, after all, one long, downhill story illustrating the inevitable mutuality between *dishonesty* with self and with others.

Remember how successful we were for a time? After convincing ourselves that we didn't have a drinking problem, how we managed to convince others? And after convincing a few compliant friends, how we then used their "evidence" to re-convince ourselves? I recall an interesting first few months when I returned from treatment, having finally found A.A. Back home, I began telling a few close friends that I was an alcoholic and had joined Alcoholics Anonymous. Guess what? You know, I'm sure, how a lot of people are about A.A. anyway. Well, several of my erstwhile friends tried hard to convince me that I wasn't "really" an alcoholic (can you hear their tone of voice?) — and they gave back to me all the arguments and "proofs" that I had fed them over the years! We really need our sponsors — someone with whom we have established a relationship of honesty — especially during such beginnings.

"Those who deceive themselves are obliged to deceive others. It is impossible for me to maintain a false picture of myself unless I falsify your picture of yourself and me."[11] Yes — and our alcoholic experience also teaches us the complementary truth: "Those who deceive others are obliged to deceive themselves. It is impossible for me to project a false picture of myself unless I falsify my own picture of me and of you." The quotation below portrays what I have come to understand about this aspect of my alcoholism much better than I could:

> As a child grows gradually aware of the absolute separateness of his being from all others in the world, he discovers that this condition offers both pleasure and terror. . . . To the extent that he must — or believes that he must — toy with his own presentation of himself to others to earn the attention and approval he craves. . . he will experience a queer, unnamable apprehension. . . This uneasy state is both painful and corrupting.
>
> It is commonly believed that this pain and corruption are consequences of his low self-esteem and fear of others' indifference and rejection, that these cause him to project himself falsely. It seems more likely that once this habit begins to harden, the crucial source of pain *is* his corruption. In his constant inability or unwillingness to tell the truth about who he is, he knows himself in his heart to be faking.
>
> Not merely is he ashamed of having and harboring a secret, unlovely, illegitimate self. The spiritual burden of not appearing as the person he "is," or not "being" the person

50

he appears to be — the extended and deliberate confusion of seeming and being — is by and large intolerable if held in direct view. If the integrity he craves is to be denied him, at least he will have its illusion. If he cannot publicize his private self. . . then he will command his private self to conform to the public one. This beguiles to a *loss* of truth; not only "telling" it, but *knowing* it.

There are some things it is impossible both to do and at the same time to impersonate oneself doing. Speaking truthfully is one of them.[12]

As often now, in sobriety, as I have meditated on that description, a new tingle of recognition goes through me each time I re-read it. Those words touch deeply and sharply one precise shame of my alcoholism: its vicious circle of dishonesty. I have learned in A.A., from A.A., that it is necesary to avoid self-deception if one is to be honest with others, and that at the same time one must be honest with others if one is to avoid self-deception. One great gift that I have received from Alcoholics Anonymous is the vision that this circle of mutuality need not be "vicious." If there is a mutuality between dishonesty with self and with others, there is also a mutuality between *honesty* with self and with others. The key to breaking the vicious circle of alcoholic dishonesty is the honest admission, "I am an alcoholic."

Our honesty in sobriety, of course, reaches far beyond that first admission. Our alcoholic dishonesty when drinking, after all, extended far beyond our denial of alcoholism. One reason why Alcoholics Anonymous works so effectively is that its meetings furnish an ideal format for reaffirming and extending that first honesty with self and with others. The honesty of each, at an A.A. meeting, enables the honesty of all. Among you, I cannot be dishonest, with you or with myself. You do not let me, for you need my honesty as I need yours. And our honesty, established in this way, grows, touching ever wider areas of each of our lives. A much-maligned modern philosopher has called the "bad faith" of self-deception the ultimate sin. Living the A.A. program, within the A.A. fellowship, delivers us from its evil.

Dishonesty becomes a habit, an addiction as tenacious and as treacherous as alcoholism itself. If I am to find the real me, I need your honesty. I need your honesty in order to find my own. And one reason I love going to A.A. meetings is that I sense that you have the same need. Because you need my honesty as I need yours, we all give by getting and get by giving.

I'd like to conclude this chapter by sharing with you another honest secret about the real me. Because children are so honest and simple, I love to read children's books. In one of them, Margery Williams's *The Velveteen Rabbit,* I came across something about being "real" that I think pretty well sums up how A.A. works for me as far as being real is concerned.

Early in the story, the young Velveteen Rabbit asks another toy, a wise, old Skin Horse, "What is REAL? . . . Does it hurt?"

> "Sometimes," said the Skin Horse, for he was always truthful. "When you are Real you don't mind being hurt."
>
> "Does it happen all at once, like being wound up," the Velveteen Rabbit asked, "or bit by bit?"
>
> "It doesn't happen all at once," said the Skin Horse. "You become. It takes a long time. That's why it doesn't often happen to people who break easily, or have sharp edges, or who have to be carefully kept. Generally, by the time you are Real, most of your hair has been loved off, and your eyes drop out and you get loose in the joints and very shabby. But these things don't matter at all, because once you are Real you can't be ugly, except to people who don't understand."[13]

I love Alcoholics Anonymous because I find in A.A. people who *do* understand. And A.A.'s greatest gift to me, after sobriety, I like to think and to hope, has been to help me become not only REAL, but someone who also understands.

Dependence and Independence

Both mutualities already examined — those of making a difference and of honesty with self and with others — flow into the third mutuality taught and enabled by Alcoholics Anonymous: that between personal dependence and personal independence.

As with the earlier mutualities, A.A.'s insight into the necessary connection between dependence and independence derives from its intuition that the reality of essential limitation is the first truth of the human condition. It is because the human is somehow the juncture of the infinite with the limited — because to be human is to be both angel and beast, "a god who shits"[14] — that human dependence and human independence must be mutually related, not only *between* people, but *within* each person. Mutuality means that each enables and fulfills the other.

To speak of a mutuality between dependence and independence, then, is to point out not only that *both* are necessary within human experience, but also that *each* becomes fully human and humanizing only by connection with the other.

Remember the image and its message, explored earlier, "Humbly on our knees"? A.A.'s mandate and caution to the alcoholic are one and the same: "You can do something, but not everything." To be human is to be in a *middle* position, and therefore to combine rather than to choose between dependence and independence. When we were drinking, we alternated between the defiant claim, "I can do it alone," and the desperate plea, "Please do it for me." Sobriety means putting aside both of those cries and accepting not only that we ourselves must do *something,* but that we need others in order to be able to do even that "something." The sober alcoholic learns in Alcoholics Anonymous both to acknowledge dependence and to exercise responsible independence. When, for whatever reason, the thought of chemical relief crosses my mind, it is *I* who pick up the *telephone* instead of the bottle — that's responsible independence. But it is the *telephone* that I pick up — and that acknowledges my dependence, my need for others.

Too many other therapies — the therapies at least that I tried before finding A.A. — look down upon the A.A. way because they prefer to interpret personal dependence and personal independence as contradictory rather than as mutually fulfilling. Their goal of independence for the alcoholic is not unrelated to their ideal of "objectivity," which leads them to ignore mutuality, and to their hope of *curing,* which stands in the way of their *caring.* Yet, as we have seen, as alcoholics we gain the freedom to not-drink only by acknowledging that our problem is not *dependence* on alcohol, but dependence on *alcohol.*

The Alcoholics Anonymous model of mutuality and caring works because it rescues alcoholics from the dire need and the doomed effort to deny all dependence. A.A. members, because they accept their essential limitation as humans, come to understand that dependence demeans and dehumanizes only if that which is depended upon is less than human. It seems to be a law of human growth that we become what we depend upon. Our choice as alcoholic human beings is not between dependence and independence, but whether we shall be dependent on a less than human substance such as booze, or on a more than individual reality such as our "Higher Power" however understood. And most of us, I think, find at least the best evidence of our "Higher Power" in others — especially in other alcoholics.

In the A.A. understanding, the truly mature person is characterized not by "independence," but rather by what some psychiatrists have termed "ontological security." For the person so secured, "dependence or independence do not become conflicting issues, rather they are complementary."[15] Such a person finds relatedness with others potentially gratifying and fulfilling.

The "ontologically insecure person" described by these therapists, on the other hand, closely resembles the active alcoholic. Having failed to come to terms with the complementarity of dependence and independence, such a person becomes preoccupied with *preserving* rather than fulfilling the self. Obsessed with the task of preserving, the ontologically insecure person reaches out to others in *self*-seeking dependency, out of the same needs that drive the alcoholic or addict to seek chemical relief.

Let me try to illustrate from my own story, which contained many attempts to treat my alcoholism through the more classic therapies. Those efforts proved unfruitful until I discovered *their* fulfillment in Alcoholics Anonymous. Several therapists suggested to me, as Dr. Harry Tiebout had pointed out to Bill Wilson, that the alcoholic seems to be fixated as a perpetual infant. The alcoholic is like the newborn infant whose cries are meant to enforce the demands of grandiose omnipotence — "His Majesty the Baby," in Tiebout's Freudian phrase.

Periodically for the alcoholic, however, as for the baby, the pinchings of reality push this sense of grandiose omnipotence to its opposite extreme. The self-pity of the hurting alcoholic echoes the implicit complaint of early childhood after the individual becomes aware of his or her relative powerlessness in a world of mature adults. From the demanding claim, "I am everything," the disillusioned alcoholic — like the helpless child — moves to the lament, "I am nothing." This understanding reflects, I think, the "very special worm" insight that we explored earlier.

Before I found A.A., my therapists all tried to convince me that maturity meant accepting the middle between "I am everything" and "I am nothing." Maturity, that is, meant embracing the realization that the proper affirmation for human beings runs, "I am something." I tried to accept that, to live it — oh how I tried! The trouble was that when things went well, I tended to lean on the first syllable — to think and to act out the sense "*I* am something." And when things were not going well, when reality pinched, I was inclined to add a word that signaled my alcoholic exceptionalism: "I am something *else*" expressed a demand that implicitly denied essential limitation. In both cases, it seemed logical and even necessary to turn again to alcohol — either to sustain the self-centered inflation of "*I*" or to enforce the self-centered exclusiveness of "something *else.*"

Alcoholics Anonymous, when I finally found it, suggested a further growth, a different maturity. Because it sees "selfishness — self-centeredness" as "the root of our troubles," because also of its sensitivity to the alcoholic as human being rather than as object, A.A. offered me an alternative to "being something." In its fellowship, I learned, I was to become someone. "I am someone" reflects more accurately human reality as essentially limited. "Someone" invites a double accent, thus removing all emphasis from the "I."

Because I learned in A.A. to accept being *some*-one, I no longer needed to try to be all; nor did I need to complain of being nothing. Both infantile claims of my alcoholic personality were closed off. Because I embraced being "some-*one*," I became able to fulfill and to be fulfilled by others, rather than threatening or being threatened by *their* individuality. I thus began to live the joyous pluralism of complementarity that has been pointed out as the essential dynamic of Alcoholics Anonymous: "the shared honesty of mutual vulnerability openly acknowledged."

The concept of "*some-one*-ness" really helps me to see the inherent mutuality of being human as a sober alcoholic in Alcoholics Anonymous. I cannot be *either* wholly dependent *or* wholly independent. To be human is to be *both* independent and dependent, and because both, neither totally. I can achieve true independence only by acknowledging real dependence. Similarly, I am able to be dependent in a truly *human* way only if I also exercise real independence. My independence is enabled and enriched by my dependence.

Once I heard an A.A. speaker suggest that in a sense we "charge batteries" by periodically acknowledging dependence. It is that acknowledgment that allows our independent operation. And, the speaker went on to point out, the other side of the image is just as true. We can't be only dependent and never exercise independence, for that would be like over-charging a battery that is never used: it would destroy both the dependent self and the charging source. The trouble with this image is that it implies some sort of "either-or" sequence. In human reality, among us as members of Alcoholics Anonymous, dependence and independence do not so much alternate as reciprocate. Our needs for dependence and independence are not met one after each other, but at the same time, in such a way that they mutually reinforce each other even as they mutually satisfy each other.

Note how well A.A. teaches and enables this, not only by its suggestion that we have some "Higher Power," but even in the way that its program and meetings work. The very First Step of the Alcoholics Anonymous program already contains the whole point here and establishes the foundation for its deeper understanding. Only by admitting that we are powerless over — and therefore dependent upon — alcohol, do we achieve the independence of freedom from addiction to alcohol.

The mutuality between personal dependence and personal independence, which we have explored in this chapter, also aids our deeper understanding of the A.A. emphasis on *limited* control and *limited* dependence. It is similar to the difference between "I cannot drink" and "I *can* not-drink"; and the distinction between "*dependence* on alcohol" or "dependence on *alcohol*." If those suggestions rang true then, I hope that you now share my vision of why they are true. Each is true because the other is true. As I learn so often in A.A., in so many ways, I am real because I am limited, just as I am limited because I am real.

All that may sound strange — even weird. Yet, if you have been where I have been, and of course you have, I think you understand. Remember? The agonizing over whether to drink at all in a situation in which we fear that there might not be "enough"? For us, when we were actively drinking, was there *ever* "enough"? The double falsity, then, of saying "No," or of "protecting our supply" when, for example, unexpected guests dropped in over a holiday when the liquor stores were closed? Were we *ever* "real" when, denying limitation, we thus played false? Or how about the games of hiding from ourselves? One of my favorites was to "cut down" by buying fifths instead of quarts;

only I made sure that the fifths — do notice the plural — were of one hundred proof instead of eighty proof.

Today, sober, I no longer have to play such games. Accepting that I am an alcoholic, accepting that I am essentially limited, I have found the reality of my dependence and of my need. I have also found — or at least am in the process of finding — the reality of myself: and *that* is *real* "independence."

Conclusion

I am an alcoholic. Accepting that, I can be myself. And strange as that may seem to some, impossible as that was when I was actively drinking, I like it. In fact, I love it so much that I wouldn't exchange it for anything else, and because it is the most precious thing I have, it is what I have tried to share with you in these pages. I hope that by your reading them we have both gained by giving, given by gaining. I know that I have; so — thank you. I would like to share with you in conclusion, and out of gratitude, something that I came across recently. Its author called it "an alcoholic's meditation on honesty; pain, and shame":

> Honesty involves exposure: the exposure of self-as-feared that leads to the discovery of self-as-is. Both of these selves are essentially vulnerable: to be is to be able to hurt and to be hurt. But something tells us that we should not

hurt: that we should neither hurt others nor hurt within ourselves. Yet we do — both hurt and hurt, both cause and feel pain.

When we cause pain, we experience guilt; when we feel pain, we suffer shame. The pain, the hurt, the guilt of the first is overt: it exists outside of us, "objectively." The pain, the hurt, the shame of the second is hidden: it gnaws within, it is "subjective." Neither can be healed without confronting the other. A bridge is needed — a connection between the hurt that we cause and the hurt that we are.

That bridge cannot be built alone. The honesty that is its foundation must be shared. A bridge cannot have only one end. Without sharing, there can be no bridge. But a bridge needs a span as well as foundations. This bridge's span is vulnerability — the capacity to be wounded, the ability to know hurt. "I need" because "I hurt" — if deepest need is honest. What I need is another's hurt, another's need. Such a need on my part would be "sick" — *if* the other had not the same need of me, of my hurt and my need. Because we share hurt, we can share healing. Because we know need, we can heal each other.

Our mutual healing will be not the healing of curing, but the healing of caring. To heal is to make whole. Curing makes whole from the outside: it is good healing, but it cannot touch my deepest need, my deepest hurt — my shame, the dread of myself that I harbor within. Caring makes whole from within: it reconciles me to myself-as-I-am — not-God, beast-angel, *human.* Caring enables me to touch the joy of living that is the other side of my shame, of my not-God-ness, of my humanity.

But I can care, can become whole, only if you care enough — need enough — to share your shame with me.

Could the same be true for you? It has been for me. Thank you for your time and your sobriety, for the hurt and the need that led you to read these pages. It is my prayer that my need and my hurt, which moved me to write these pages, may help to heal yours and you.

FOOTNOTES

[1]"4. Made a searching and fearless moral inventory of ourselves.
8. Made a list of all persons we had harmed, and became willing to make amends to them all.
9. Made direct amends to such people wherever possible, except when to do so would injure them or others."

[2]"5. Admitted to God, to ourselves, and to another human being the exact nature of our wrongs.
6. Were entirely ready to have God remove all these defects of character.
7. Humbly asked Him to remove our shortcomings."

[3]Quoted by Lucien Goldman, *The Hidden God* (New York: Humanities Press, 1964), p. 188.

[4]Quoted by Morton and Lucia White, *The Intellectual Versus the City* (New York: Mentor, 1964), p. 188.

[5]Ernest Becker, *The Denial of Death* (New York: Free Press, 1973), p. 58.

[6]H. J. Almond, "Moral Re-Armament: The Oxford Group," unpublished Master's thesis, Yale University, 1947, p. 12.

[7]Quoted by Helen Merrell Lynd, *On Shame and the Search for Identity* (New York: Harcourt, Brace, & World, 1958), pp. 29-30.

[8]*Alcoholics Anonymous* (A.A. World Services, Inc.: New York, 1976 rev. ed.), p. 185.

[9]R. D. Laing, *Self and Others* (Baltimore: Pelican, 1971), p. 136.

[10]Andras Angyal, quoted by Milton Mayeroff, *On Caring* (New York: Harper & Row Perennial, 1971), frontispiece.

[11]Laing, *Self and Others*, p. 143.

[12]Leslie H. Farber, *Lying, Despair, Jealousy, Envy, Sex, Suicide, Drugs, and the Good Life* (New York: Basic Books, 1976), pp. 196-198.

[13]Margery Williams, *The Velveteen Rabbit* (New York: Doubleday, 1958).

[14]Becker, *The Denial of Death*, p. 58.

[15]This line of thought is best summarized by Harry Guntrip, *Psychoanalytic Theory, Therapy, and the Self* (New York: Basic Books, 1971); cf. especially pp. 115, 118, 126, 190.